W9-CPD-971

Jaguar Rain

the Margaret Mee Poems

also by Jan Conn

Red Shoes in the Rain
The Fabulous Disguise of Ourselves
South of the Tudo Bem Café
What Dante Did with Loss
Beauties on Mad River

Jaguar Rain

the Margaret Mee Poems

Jan Conn

Preface by Sir Peter Crane
Director, Royal Botanic Gardens, Kew

Brick Books

Library and Archives Canada Cataloguing in Publication

Conn, Jan, 1952-
    Jaguar rain : the Margaret Mee poems / Jan Conn ;
preface by Sir Peter Crane.

Includes bibliographical references.
ISBN-13: 978-1-894078-48-1
ISBN-10: 1-894078-48-9

1. Mee, Margaret—Poetry. I. Mee, Margaret II. Title.

PS8555.O543J34 2006   C811'.54   C2005-907691-7

We acknowledge the Canada Council for the Arts, the
Government of Canada through the Book Publishing Industry
Development Program (BPIDP), and the Ontario Arts
Council for their support of our publishing program.

Cover image: *Cattleya violacea*, 1981. Margaret Mee. Rio Cuini,
Amazonas state, Brazil. Royal Botanic Gardens, Kew.

The author photograph is by Carl Schlichting.

The book is set in Bembo, Rotis and Zapfino.

Design and layout by Alan Siu.

Printed by Sunville Printco Inc.

Brick Books
431 Boler Road, Box 20081
London, Ontario N6K 4G6

www.brickbooks.ca

IN MEMORIAM

Herbert Murray Keith Conn (1923-2004)

Anne Halley (1928-2004)

for Carlo

for Greville and Elisabeth Mee

Contents

The Light on the Rio Maturacá

Translating Yellows

Wildlife

Eel and Storm

Illustrations

Cover: *Cattleya violacea*, 1981. Margaret Mee. Rio Cuini, Amazonas state, Brazil. Royal Botanic Gardens, Kew.

Antecedents: Ink sketch of map of River Araçá, north of the Rio Negro. Journey dated 1970. Margaret Mee. Royal Botanic Gardens, Kew.

AKA Heaven: *Clusia grandifolia*, 1982. Margaret Mee. Rio Negro, Amazonas state, Brazil. Royal Botanic Gardens, Kew.

The Light on the Rio Maturacá: *Streptocalyx poeppigii*, 1985. Margaret Mee. Amazonas state, Brazil. Royal Botanic Gardens, Kew.

Translating Yellows: *Catasetum galeritum*, 1981. Margaret Mee. Amazonas state, Brazil. Royal Botanic Gardens, Kew.

Wildlife: Unknown plant, possibly Ochnaceae family, 1972. Margaret Mee. Rio Jurubaxi, Amazonas state, Brazil. Royal Botanic Gardens, Kew.

Eel and Storm: *Sobralia margaretae*, 1977. Margaret Mee. Rio Urupadi, Amazonas state, Brazil. Royal Botanic Gardens, Kew.

ROYAL
BOTANIC
GARDENS
KEW

PLANTS PEOPLE
POSSIBILITIES

The rainforest of Amazonia teems with an exuberance of plant and animal life. Here heliconias, orchids, bromeliads and aroids flourish in a seemingly limitless tangle of trees, interrupted only by great rivers that flow to far away oceans. Nurtured by year-round warmth and an abundance of moisture, these great forests are among the most biologically diverse habitats on our planet. They have proved irresistible for some of the greatest of all explorers: Von Humboldt, Wallace, Spruce, and in the mid-twentieth century the irrepressible and extraordinarily talented artist Margaret Mee. In this book of exquisite poems, Jan Conn brings alive the wonder and mystery of Amazonia and at the same time, illuminates the thirst for exploration and knowledge that continues to attract so many to this vast green wilderness.

But it was more than just inquisitiveness that drew Mee and her predecessors into the unknown. Penetrating the rainforest is also an emotional experience. And just as Margaret Mee's evocative images showed us the rainforest in new ways, *Jaguar Rain* connects us with its sights, sounds, smells and tastes to evoke a vivid picture of plants, animals, people and a single, extraordinary spirit. Through the rich images in these poems Margaret Mee's travels and experiences are brought to life in ways that even the most dramatic narrative could not match. They remind us of what is important about one of the last great natural places on Earth.

Jan Conn deserves all our thanks for a work of remarkable expressiveness that brings Margaret Mee's life into new focus. I'm sure you will enjoy taking this journey with them.

Professor Sir Peter Crane FRS

Director
Royal Botanic Gardens, Kew

Antecedents

Near the Solimões River, 1880

What would *you* do, she asked, if you came upon a man
wearing eight black-necked red cotingas around his waist?
Their heads and tails scarlet. Everything else glossy, buffed
black. A bar tips the tail like a blackout over the eyes of
torture victims in police photographs.

As he walks toward me, a strange arrhythmic sound: snail
shell and animal bone on his chest rubbing together. The
feathers brush against me first, then other things. Bird feet,
claws clenched.

Bowl and Spear

She is handed a charred wooden bowl in the form of a
double-headed jaguar. It bares its teeth. Then a spear,
turquoise-feathered—an auspicious colour. Damaged on the
boat to Europe from the Upper Rio Negro.

She is not a warrior, she claims. (A well-known delaying
tactic.) *What then*, they query, hiding her notebook under a
tree. *Tukano, volcano*, she murmurs as if making an offering.
Heat it up. Ask for crimson. Put on the armadillo mask, dash
into the forest.

Casa de Pedra

On a flat rock wall, six red-pigmented stick figures, human.
The rock yellowish, scored with black cracks. Hazardous,
perhaps. Dream-like, the figures wait. Who can look them in
the eye (blood-red)?

He heats and stirs the mineral pigments, fans the flames with
a palm leaf. *Hold hands*, he says, conspiring with his subjects
in the flickers of light. Then hurries to join them.

The House of the Tapir

Into the House of the Tapir no one goes. Woven into its walls, nightblack and amber motifs become anaconda gliding along a branch of water, jaguar loping across the savannah. The shaman waits at the entrance, in a dream or trance.

Carrying manioc in a basket, feet set on a red dirt path, the boy pauses. The war trumpet sounds a second time, shuddering the earth. He will be hunted down.

Breathlessly, he slips into the House. Scent of dried arumã fills his head. Long after midnight, he sits down on the carved spirit seat, forbidden to him. Flies away into the darkness.

Pacoval Incised

Turtle puzzles over its rounded shell, inserts of cracked hexagon. It thinks: round contains, hexagons are edged. Sharp, pointy. Things fall off them.

Meanwhile the river licks turtle's lips and a lazy man is hung upside down from a ceiba tree. As blood rushes to his brain, new ideas form as clouds, then dissipate.

Watching the clouds come and go, turtle stands on its head but new ideas are a long time coming.

Charm against Personal Fears

He wants his own ears back, not these jaguar ears, brilliant red. He has about 60 teeth in his mouth, identical glossy rectangles like keys from a dismembered piano. He wants his own teeth back.

Bolivar! He screams, but he really means *Rodrigues Ferreira!* (who collected the thing). Out of his mouth crawls a giant anaconda.

The eco-tour guide shrugs: choose the "extreme transformation," showing off for your girl—it happens every time. His runs away with the stunt man from *The African Queen.*

First Contact: Scissors

The boys and men of tribe X liked to fish along the rocky tributaries of the Tapajós for giant pirarucú. They meticulously cleaned the razor-sharp scales (now made into jewellery) and put them aside for a feast honouring the passage into manhood, roasted the flesh.

Then came scissors. In black and white we witness the crude clipping of thick ebony hair. The gangly "barber" is a travelling salesman. Fish scales are passé, he informs the assembled tribe. For the scissors (three pairs) he "accepts" 2,500 sq km of their land. (No fish in this photograph.)

AKA Heaven

The Rain Holds Its Breath

In a small room with flint-blue walls, a woman
studies a rare orchid, its Nile-green leaves
propped open, lustrous. Smelling of damp,
her sketchbook opens beside her.

The room quietly fills with a fine
ivory mist. Someone knocks at the door;
the leaves fall from her fingers. Fairies
from her British childhood, tiny

among the orchid buds, rustle out of sight.
The sound of flowers opening, she thinks.
Rubs her eyes. The buds are shut tight.
From behind the door the fairies

waft toward her a fragrance glorious
as ten thousand lilies. The rain holds its breath.

For the Giant Anteater

Heat slaps our faces, a wet white sheet, under the massive mango trees

I trade my gouache for the giant anteater, its long viscous tongue

Pre-dawn, down a hundred wooden steps into thick mist, hidden river

When scarlet ibis float across the molten greens, suns also rise

We cross rapids: eyes wide open, swinging long bamboo, poling by
heart

You who fear ceiling spiders, invite them into your hammock

Night spirits, Candomblé, a cock dies—coral snake on my path today

Luscious pink and cream petals fall: the giddy yellow core

Inky clouds, threatening sky: how low in the water our dugout

I cannot save the lemon trees from the woman with the evil eye

In the igarapé, euphonious bells of the lily chime, chime

Mangrove roots, black mud, little crabs—boiled on board in a
blackened pot

Ticks desert the band of skinny pigs: on us grow fat as red balloons

Rio Guamá

All along the dark purple river, the egrets
stop feeding as the barge of red-

and-ochre painted humans churns to a stop.
Gracefully, silently, the birds rise

and disappear above the trees. People scramble from the barge,
flounder in the shallows, trying to follow the birds.

We pause, rewind. Notice now
the swollen faces under thin layers of dried clay,

the twisted, broken spears. With a flick
the image is gone. Outside the screened windows,

rain pours down. A shroud envelops
the world, the river empties itself of images.

Gustavia augusta

My dank toes are
hidden in the red earth,
my flower's centre like a radioactive
lion's ruff, hot, sparking.

Blossoms, at my base, oyster-shell white then
towards the tips, pink, pinker, pinkest!
If white is all colours, then pink
is white squeezed to its edges,

white ^{cubed}, without the straitjacket.

Moon with Ant

i

buzojy tuk bwikiserehe:

    iki, tsy

ii

natsi orobik, tsumy pihik;

    sokoro tsapu

        pyryhyk pyrysuk

iii

zuma zo
    jokba je mukto

i

moon with ant:

    older sister, younger brother

ii

corn arrow, honey water

    capybara tooth

        snake shoe

iii

to feel once again
    small mother fruit

Alto Juruena

Beyond the palm thatch maloca a large porcupine
crouches in the canopy of stars, and a garden

of animal skulls on sticks—tapir, jaguar,
monkey, possum. Moon noise. The floor littered

with ashes. Her hair pulled back with elaborate red and
ebony combs, a young woman peels yams, smiles from

broken teeth. Near the igarapé, fish walk on fins
to lay eggs in the mud. The river enters my dreams

as do the monstrous ridged stones in their groups along
the banks, covered with rose-pink water plants

lovely and flawless, but not those I seek.

The Rikbaktsa

A coati races, screaming, through the middle
of the camp.
Bands of yellow caciques
surround me, screech at my feet,
each sporting Mr. Universe shoulders
the colour of ripening mangoes.

The caboclo visitors are worse than disease—
gorging on river turtle they've roasted alive,
their children illiterate evangelists.

Why should *they* care about the Rikbaktsa
with their distended earlobes
curled around wooden discs,
tiny wives who wear nothing
but beads

—even though they create sparks from tinder, a wooden spindle,
and shimmering cobalt air.

>   *After a two-day manhunt, all the exhausted anthropologist can say
>   by midnight is, Pass the peccary, would you please?*

Now I won't have to marry the brutal
rubber-collector—
all that's left of *him*
is three small teeth.

Aripuana

Will the boat come back for me? Nights
on this rocky island a possum steals my fish,

and the phosphorescent eyes of a coral shark slide
back and forth across the sandy shallows, sleepless,

ravenous. Days I watch wasps
construct paper nests like miniature pots,

the hinged lids ingenious. When the jaguar appears
I am nearly fearless: on the river bank I have discovered

the rare lemon-yellow beauty, *Oncidium cebolleta*. My terror now
is leaf-cutting ants. If they find the wooden racks I've built

for my orchids and bromeliads, they'll devour my life.

Blue Silk

I follow in the small overloaded canoe
all morning paddling hard, with the child José
navigating rapids from the bow.

    Light like a bell.
    River of blue silk, blue silk, blue silk.

I know precisely where we are,
near the tip of one forested island among many,
tiny specks on the Rio Alto Juruena.

    Giant otter, tapir, ocelot, slip off their pelts
    on the riverbank, fly to a rendezvous in the sky.

José knows the single safe channel
through turbulent water and black rocks omnipotent
as thunderheads. He never hesitates.

    At dusk, golden pleasure flowers close—
    stars seduce the night lilies, all passion and perfume.

I compose a letter to Greville: in the event of death by
   drowning
wrap me in flower petals and lianas,
fiery citron song of the sun.

AKA Heaven

The troubled moon stutters up behind the trees, slender and antiseptic
as though fighting a chronic disease. Long after the insects cease
rasping and creaking, the phallic bract of a bromeliad
shyly opens from its prickly base, vermilion and magenta
lighting the moist rainforest dark.

Do bromeliads have souls, like the great silent trees?
Are they firecracker or demurely green?

Pre-dawn and the moon has faltered—
sun steals the scene. But even the satin streaks of daybreak
can't compete with the ranks of lavender eyelash
and primal curve, a shriek of colour loud as the scarlet macaw
calling above the palms. Bird and bromeliad might be brothers,

straining recklessly for the extraordinary tinted blue,
high and beyond reach overhead, also known as heaven.

Serra do Curicuriari

I scale the Serra in a grey sharkskin suit,
chartreuse leather gloves. South, alabaster birds wheel

in and out of a massive thunderhead. Huge storm tonight,
another one tomorrow. I wave and call to my husband

in São Paulo. At my feet, the filigree of a waterfall:
scarlet heliconias two metres tall and a cloud

of pure white orchids. *I must be dreaming.*
From the mist emerges a flaming orange

cock-of-the-rock. We eye each other.
Plummeting like a flare dropped he dives

into the black heart of the river. I follow him down.

Small Pink Nebulae

The diamond wash, the diamond wash—carry me with you, little gems

Peer through the window into forest—green demons weep, tear out their hair

Moon strolls through closed doors into ant's nuptial chamber, uninvited guest

Little capuchins swing upside down in the rippling fountains of leaves

Carrying stars on their shoulders, coatis pause, wide-eyed, for a drink

Inside the woman's lucent body dwell cloud-fish, small pink nebulae

It is not my turn to do headstands in the eel's house of the water

On a break from corralling caiman, he applies crimson lipstick

Above cliffs of granite, ancestors hover: flash of lightning, clouds burst

My snake spirit lies down with a painted clay doll, what rises in the night

Clusia field sketch

Exquisite petals, swirl
of a full-length ball gown
        swept, whirled,

pulled between two partners
until, exhausted, she bows out,
        or leans, as here, drooping

but outwardly flamboyant still,
arms sheathed in vermilion gloves,
        gown propped against the olive-green stem.

Blossom eats its own red.

King of the Amazon

Behind Salvador's house in São Felipe—
        enormous ancient clusia trees.
        Their purple-bronze petals float

lazily down the Rio Içana like poems
        set adrift by Li Po
        hundreds of years ago.

At twilight I can see
        into the lunar depths of the river.
        With a shimmer Venus rises,

pulling up the crescent moon.
        In the dark hollows at the base of the tree
        the bushmaster, sleek and cool

glides through the undergrowth,
        King of the Amazon.
        His bite is fatal. What I want is nothing to him.

The Light on the Rio Maturacá

Commodus on the Cauaburi

The cut branch and the sloth fall to the deck, his long claws
click click click on the wooden boards. After him tumbles

the showy blue orchid, scarlet-lipped and eager
for a night on the town. We are told the story

of the boat owner who collected too many sloths
for a film, tossed the extras to the captured jaguars,

imagining himself Commodus at the Roman Coliseum,
cheering as they were torn to shreds.

Indigo clouds, stippled with amber, gather in the west.
The nightjars swoop across the archipelago of small islands,

scissored tails flickering like souls of the newly dead,
silver, shining.

Mountain of Mist and Cloud

When I exhale, mist rises above the ebony waterways.
So I must be a god, albeit
minor. A mountain god?

No one ascends Pico da Neblina
without the requisite guides—
recklessly I invoke secret charms.

Richard Spruce never climbed this one:
I shall be the first European
up the southern approach.

But south—bad luck?
I fear the crimson of the road to the south,

how the tint of it drowns,
dissipates in still water.
Our whole expedition slowly

submerging. Must I bind two scarlet arara feathers
to my upper arms, like the Waika men,
to scale this blue-black

voracious hunk of granite?
Will it feed on me?

In the village the shaman
steams in the midday sun.
Painted black serpents writhe across his chest.

In his eyes, I see some dark shape
crawling blindly forward
on hands and knees.

Someone in the crowd plaits
and unplaits my unruly blonde hair.

What am I doing here?

I thought I resembled a flower,
silk, raw silk, but unravelling, petal
after petal. Down to the core.

Here's the core, is it brilliant yellow?
Is this the one they call Margaret?
Shall I lift my carnelian skirts

and begin the ascent?

Pico da Neblina

On the steep climb to the summit, the faces
of Waika killed by influenza
float, blue among the clouds.

The ambrosial fruit of the papaya, planted
at the borders of the maloca, couldn't save them. God

is in the clearings, not the forest. Rafael points to a marked tree
near his father's burial site. He cannot go back

to the mission, or transform the moon into a white disk
to tame and wear on his tongue. He becomes

the ravenous jaguar, roaming the hillsides.
Spirits sucking his bones the feiticeiro cannot cure.

Why

weep when the path to the summit is washed out?
      Bromeliads relish the rain.
Why cry when food runs low?
      Giant earthworms make a great stir-fry.

With fresh-cut leaves, re-roof the old shelter.
      Light a small fire, feast on papaya.

Better to cry over the abandoned malocas,
      their families buried beneath our feet.
Better to weep on the way back down, knee-deep in mud.
      Send the hunters into the woods

for a votive termite nest to toss on the flames.
      Taste the amber smoke, the bitter smoke.

The Santa Casa

…and I am on the hospital terrace, painting *Catasetum*,
each flower a red-eyed spirit mask topped with an extravagant

five-petaled chapeau, one-of-a-kind Rio creation.
The room where I sleep is massive and dark, uninhabited

since patients from the epidemic walked
or were carried away. All night a vampire bat flits between

my mosquito net and the parrot's wooden cage, terror in its
small sharp teeth. Outside the forest is streaked with a chaos

of flashlight beams, transforming leaves into phantasmagorical
shapes. The novelty delights the Waika, who for these cheap

metal torches traded their elegant feather earrings.
Beyond the mission walls, a man who lost his wife to measles

wails, calling down the stars from the far away
night sky, to plunge into the river and drown.

The Monkey-Skin Bracelet and I

We are watching, the monkey-skin bracelet and I,
      for the river to narrow, rocky banks to loom
perilous because of shadows, shallows.
        Trees viewed by torchlight loose their astonished souls.

We are watching the heavy grey drizzle—
      it seeps inside our minds, leaving black stains of genipapo
on our skin. In the dark the caiman's red eyes
      sparkle, primitive. Lure us down to the river.

We are watching the preparation of plantain soup.
      Add the ashes of the chieftain's wife,
shavings of moonlight, a pinch of that uranium rain,
      night perfume: her soul will not come back.

The Curious Waistcoat of the Armadillo

I would like to stay here, under the giant tree,
above the rapids on the Rio Marauiá, where no one comes

to fix the electrical wires, and the telephone
never rings. The clusia are ripe

raspberry-red inside and ivory outside, translucent
as porcelain. I'm better here than I will be

in London, on exhibit with my paintings. The chieftain
wants to cut my frizzy blonde hair and colour it red with urucu.

Here, the spirits live close to the ground, in the coati
with his marvellous silver-and-black-striped tail, in the curious

waistcoat of the armadillo. And at the end of every day,
the wind and the roar of the rapids carry everything away.

Translating Yellows

Voice of Flowers

West of Manaus, past Coarí, the flooded landscape
is a maze of islets and single trees, violet clouds

and bold unsettling moonshadows. Slicing a trail
through the water, copper fin of a peixe-cachorro

leads us to the village of Alvaraes. *Dog-fish! How I adore
your sturdy, ugly body, lightly armoured with glittering scales,*

head like a salmon skull...

Massive gourds droop from the calabash tree,
half-submerged like buoys, speaking in glottal stops

where the river twists and eddies.
By starlight we discover chickens inhabiting a canoe.

The river god rows past, singing with a voice of flowers.

Orchid and Sandpiper

Lime-green lipped, still-tongued,
 burgundy-striped in a small hint
of natural selection's occasional hysteria.
 Araken detected it, paddled
his canoe uncannily into the ferny,
 mossy glade, richocheting
with stained-glass-window light,
 bejewelled, sparkling, a sanctuary
from the civilisados' greed, the caboclo settler
 who had just killed one of a pair
of sandpipers feeding along the river edge,
 brown speckled designer feathers
tucked around its wildly racing heart.

Amazonian Whites

Dusk. Huge panicles of egrets blossom in the kapok trees.

White-hot vats of Manaus liquid steel—
no hope there for the everlasting gesture, no hope.

Swallowing the alabaster petals. *Pass me another lily*, she says.

To hell with gold, what I want are fake quartz teeth
to tear your great big tender heart in two.

Mr. Albino is 80 but rules the Rio Demini with manic cruelty.

The sea is foaming in my little lake,
bringing a fresh school of ivory dolphins.

We're always interested in rewarding excellence, he said,
approaching her with a cream-coloured rope.

Cho-cho, you are mistaken—there are no white mammals here.

Clusia species

Ruffled pearl-white flowers, dainty lingerie.

Shining serpentine leaves buffed silver, cobalt
like little minnow backs in underwater glow—

Leaf vein seals two leaf lips shut,
white-seamed buds hang
petite baseballs amidst
the green and roaring crowds.

Up the Rio Negro

My travelling companions upriver
include a once-white kitten foaming with rabies
and its drunken owner.

The river choked with black piranhas.
I am on the Rio Negro, I remind myself,
because of longing.

My diet reduced to fish, manioc
and a single lemon a day. There is no sugar,
no serum for rabies.

Longing to let the small door of my body open
and my soul slip out.
To become a tree laden with bignonia,

trailing small pink trumpets in the inky water.
To slide behind the eye
of a jacaré, iridescent

pygmy kingfisher, or the huge snake
carelessly draped around the base of a palm.
Instead I find my long shirtsleeves soaked,

hanging over the edge of the deck,
and the kitten—
a present for a pregnant wife

awaiting her husband's return
in their isolated settlement.
He wants to surprise her.

Fish Leap toward the Moon

While we sleep uneasily, phosphorescent fish leap toward the moon

In Maués the hotels are crammed with bureaucrats
                    In the convent I sleep agnostically in my hammock

Gold spots or stars brighten the dark firmament of the tucanaré
                    I will not eat such beauty for dinner

All along the river hundreds of bronze cormorants
                    As one, they lift their wings, shout endearments to the sun

Fragrance of dried palm leaves in the old priest's hut
                    The stars light me up—I constellate, I glow

My indigo desire, my turquoise girl
                    All day I yearn to see the small blue palms

Upswept red coif, woodpecker camps it up
                    Sleek tayra remain stealthy: your skin is in danger

Each night falls like a black machete
                    Only my flashlight to keep it at bay

Translating Yellows

Night after night I shock myself with betrayals—
the water glass empty, shower of golden blossoms
cascading down my thin arms.

No longer love being tasted, brought intact into the world.

Instead, fragments, flower centre dark orange,
horsefly in amber, its wings stuck open
in a last crazed dive—

So, Mr. Moonshine, why
do these petals ache with yellow?

On the floor, a shot glass. Pickled cherry in the gin cup.

I tread softly, shattering glasses one after the other.
It's the *Death of a Salesman*, someone I
used to know once upon a time in America.

I wonder whether those Buddhist monks
who torched themselves calmly were not also dressed
in saffron or daffodil,

and the flames, visible from Pluto,
what colour were they?

Apricots burst with light. So many little stars and suns
in my basket at market I wince,

hold them at arm's length:

small and burnished, Vermeer glimmer.

Furled petals announce a breach birth. Out pop

twin shooting stars. How to mother them,
along with the sting rays,
keeps me up the next night and the night after that.

I spiral around one fixed point:
a golden shower of blossoms glimpsed along the Rio Mamori.

Sketch in one hand, prayer wheel in the other.

Mistaken for Thieves

Mistaken for thieves on the night of the Feast of Judas.
  Nobody home. We hang hammocks

from the pale-branched pau d'arco. Tormented by dreams
  of gentlemen in navy frock coats (they are not butlers).

Moonlight seeps in, silvering our limbs, the snarling half-blind
  dogs in the small enclosure next door. Now, owl,

black-beaked and hooded, sings his assassin song—
  the rodent folk are mesmerized. So much terror!

How does it fit into the plush slippers of their bodies?
  Fear in us resides back of the brain, rushing

up and down the spine like an express train.
  Owl, owl! Not now, not now.

Listen: the moon is your showboat, your roulette wheel.
  Ours too. What thieves value most: gasoline

for their clandestine travel, stranding us here with owl and terror.
  Nights without moon. Unpenned ravening dogs.

Carnelian Flowers, Dark Trees

The dark, is it self-willed or otherwise?

Barcelos has become too sophisticated
for practical footwear. I must make do
with high-heeled shoes. Pink at that.

Dark pink, I think. Uh oh. Now we're in a corner.

A wet corner, inside a prize bromeliad. With one large frog
(a good accessory to a semi-aquatic hat), swarms
of ants, red scorpions—a pair (one left, one right).

To the right, fires of a slaughterhouse pinprick the night.

I speak like the blue-green fireflies, in code.
Stealthily I rescue the howler monkeys
being sold (for meat) downstream.

Crossing the rivers of light I become incandescent.

The Maraú River: a Lament

Who stands beside me in the charred forest,
sleek and wondrous as a jaguar,
stepping ahead into the bleak darkness?

His paddle a large golden leaf across one shoulder,
red-and-ochre stain on his arms
and chest, he points ahead to a white tree in the igapó—

His voice like *Cecropia* leaves being torn
Remember the way we were, the Mauhés, before most of us
were killed by influenza or butchered by men

like the "River King." Imagine how it was before he told us
he owned every tree, all the animals hidden in the forest,
the water beneath our canoes, the whole of the Maraú River...

Wildlife

Biographies

This sketchbook and I are out all day in the jaguar rain.

Urospatha sagittifolia

One is tempted to lean forward and lick
first the moist citron inner surface of the spathe,
then the rich burgundy outside
and so uncoil the incredible frenzy of the twisted top—
fall asleep in the blue-green depths of the arrowed leaf,
follow the phloem river...

Heliconia: a triptych

I. *Heliconia chartacea* var. *meeana*

Part plesiosaur, part dancing slipper,
each bract hung with traditional
teal-blue bells—
and who or what would answer
from deep in the heart of the forest
if you rang—

II. *Heliconia chartacea*

I am the lipsticked mouths
of famous beauties, the telltale
coral or burgundy trace
left on your fancy dress shirt—
I whisper heady secrets, then
leave you hanging in a riot of scarlet and creamy magenta.

III. *Heliconia adeleana*

Inside my half-translucent bracts I've a cargo
unlike any other: tangerine fire-crackers.
Within each one a minute belly-dancer
is already swaying provocatively to the deep green
music the little female flowers are composing
with their hot sulphur lips.

Cattleya violacea

Down the tree trunk parade queens of the prom
in luscious violet-magenta—these femmes fatales
are no one's corsage!
Swish, swish of their silken underskirts, their
perfume magnified in this decadent heat
like promises in a darkened hallway,
the whole forest watching.

Nymphaea rudgeana

Undersurface of the leaf richly textured and pink
as a tongue. Five ivory flowers nearby
unlace their gowns languidly for their emperor
the sun—surely five is a sacred number
on the Rio Nhamundá?
And the burgundy and moss-green sepals
employed as eunuchs to guard the family jewels.

Scuticaria steelii

The spotted canary-yellow flowers
open their jaguar mouths:
a glimpse of brick-red jaguar throat—
the roar-box, the purr-box,
and those lovely ferocious teeth.

This elaborate orchid bracelet
circling the tree trunk begins to move,
slowly picking up speed, spinning the forest.
Every year drawing Amazonian waters higher,
maker of the várzea.

Philodendron brevispathum

Shapely spathes,
marble-white torsos flecked and stained fuchsia,
rising from the dream-blue, sea-blue stems—
they rival Michelangelo!
And curl the tips of the leaves,
their veins an emerald swirl.

Cochleanthes amazonica

Only their attendant bees notice
how each flower cascades
down the insect-riddled trunk
like a parachutist, lavishly robed,

how each radiates
fecund fuchsia light
in a rhapsody of evolution,
escapes pink-winged and fragrant
into the green void.

Glory

So endearingly, casually phallic
is the unfurling cream-coloured bloom
of the watery aninga

glimpsed from the wooden window
of the passing train I nearly swoon.
And now, as we are stopped

just past the Rio Amapari, I must make do
with a view of that lone black chicken
in a makeshift soccer pitch.

The priest in the very front
of the most expensive reserved seats
assures us this particular train

is headed straight for glory,
albeit via the city of Santana.
Glory, I think. *Haven't been there yet.*

Mist descends as a cloud or ascends
from the brilliant emerald ground.
It's never clear.

Heliconia, I'd rather sway in your
smooth citron bracts,
away down the Amapari.

Glory I find in the jumping spider, all eyes,
stalking its prey on the unknown rose-pink flower,
and the yellow-and-black-striped beetle

that lands on my shoulder and climbs
from darkness into the radiant light
of early June.

Margaret Considers von Humboldt

Vermilion sky in the west, mauve lightning coming on,
storm clouds begin to heave and crackle.
Under the jambeiro tree, little shadows gather
and creep up the side of the wall.
The lawn opens and closes like a zipper.

The dogs bark and howl at some unseen thing
whirling leaves across the grass.
What was von Humboldt thinking, wandering along
the Amazon near Belém, simultaneously plotting
the geological past of the river basin

and the capture of a pink river dolphin? The wind hums,
languidly waves its paper fan.
In another room people argue,
voices indistinct, but with that unmistakable cadence,
you you you she she she he he he, rising and falling,

and then a sound as of cold water thrown in the face.
Musing, he taps his monocle: who in Europe will believe his tales
of gigantic stingrays, fruit-eating river fish, purple geodes
where stars glimmer during the day? Absentmindedly stroking
his new beard, overheard to mutter to himself,

How I love the petals of the wind, their blue lips.

Notes from the Hotel Paris, Manaus

I want to run away
to the Rio Andirá,
away from the Hotel Paris in Manaus,
from the great southern cities
where a government hand is raised and the forests begin to burn.

I need to gather
   a few orchids in the pau d'arco,
   a few bromeliads in the igapó—

Look for me on my hand-drawn maps. I'll be paddling
hard down one of those black-water rivers, stained
with the ink from my pen.

I'll be thinking of you from my hammock, as the light
from the crescent moon delicately erodes another building
in São Paulo.

The Bay of Sapucaia

The deep light doesn't enter here, nor the angels.
It is not forbidden, but I descend from the boat
onto a swaying island of pliant grass—

and sink waist-deep into black river mud. The hoatzin
calls from its hidden nest; mosquitoes and ants
feast on me. Where is the boatman

swinging his heavy lantern, my guide with his hunting knife?
The immense anaconda glides down a dry hillside in my dream
emerging from bushes in a pool of moonlight.

Nothing can protect me: not amulet nor chant nor medicine.
But now it's daylight and I am huddled in the bow of the boat,
and nothing else matters but the oncoming storm.

To Be Sung to Villa-Lobos' "The Amazon Forest"

i

The olive-green *Epidendron* orchid, petals slender as sea-star arms, swims nightlong across the sky, creamy-white laces and ribbons creating stars and galaxies in their wake.

ii

To cure a fear of piranhas, catch and eat three every night for seven days. Then wade into the river up to your neck and wait.

iii

Where's the trombone player, the sax man? I sleep in the boat, bathe in the shade of the red cedar tree.

iv

Richard Spruce described "the loftiest falls known on the Rio Negro," noted the area's breathtakingly giant trees. We find trees gone, forest empty.

v

At dawn, wings flashing crimson then black. Toucan the skybearer carries the half-moon to the heavens in his ivory bill.

vi

By moonlight, by starlight, the manatees mate among the waterlogged ruins of Old Airão. The waters of the Rio Negro boil.

vii

To continue down the Rio Unini we must appease the
guardian of the rapids, risk treacherous underwater rocks.
Our pilot's eyesight is failing. We disguise the boat with water
plants.

Wasps

I glimpse on the Rio Unini a striking orchid:
burgundy streamers surrounding palest tourmaline.
        Between us, a mob of black wasps

expands, contracts in a furious rising cloud.
What are the rules of engagement with wasps?
        They are fearless. They have

a personality disorder. They must have been fed
raw red as larvae. Why can't they meditate
        on some calm object or concentrate

on their perfect armour, reflected in the cool
tungsten mirror of the river? Cousin to
        the curved tails of scorpions,

they are programmed as warriors, fierce and remote.
In their dark outfits they might be
        a troop of Giorgio Armani suits.

Each is the length of the first two joints of an index finger.
Their hearts are mean and pinched, or perhaps
        they have no heart at all.

Peer into their ruthless eyes. Nothing,
but very angry, stares back. As if looking
        in on black interiors

looking in on black interiors. They never sleep. Theirs
is the memoir of the insomniac,
        the one with hexagonal eyes.

Fountains of Water Blown Skyward

Into view comes the Parana do Ramos, long and thin
                    Our boat undulates between slate-green banks

Big male dolphins blow fountains of water skyward
                    I recall that I once had gills, dove deep

In a house on stilts Chief Manoel sighs and waits
                    His only lamp the moon, the star map way up high

We query caiman, older than all, or water lilies, sisters to stars
                    Should we journey in this yellow air, charged with coming storms

We land in a dark forest, among towering trees
                    Woodpecker, spare this tree, your dazzling crimson head

Grebes, herons, macaws wing past us, heading upriver
                    Trolling for some larger thing, with moon for bait

Wildlife

From a liana dangle two metres of snake.
    With this the gloomy forest attempts
to charm us (we are charmed) into entering—

I'm betting on the golden-limbed monkeys who invade my fruit trees:
    at least as many neurons as Louis Agassiz.

Curled into a russet-brown ball, the pygmy anteater.
    So young, already a genius.

As she grows her sides redden like a thousand ripening cherries. Pirarucú
    sways her scarlet tail languidly
through murky water. Breathless, we trail behind.

In aquamarine or magenta, jewelled dragonflies descend.
    The envy of angels: not even they have such intricate wings.

Green-eyed in the mango tree crouches a black onça.
    Its luminous twin in the Museo—its great heart slowly swinging shut.

Iguana nights: bony, delicate feet and hands. Face
    of an invalid. Sea-green ruffle hangs from its jaw—
in which century, dear sir, did you last practise law?

Bounding along the reddish, muddy bank, a giant otter—
    streamlined, slick—dives beneath the lily pads, among the giant fish.

I open the oropendola's straw purse—
    her eggs glow opalescent as pearls.

Rescued from a sinking boat, my hyacinth macaw
    rehearses tubercular coughs of the inebriated crew,
stutters the final *putt-putts* of the engine.

Eel and Storm

Seeking the Source of the Rio Cauhy

This former river by day is brick-red, dusty, rutted.

At dusk nightjars carry off bits in their star-speckled beaks.

By night it's black as spiders.

It meanders, deviates.

Disappears.

Eel and Storm

From the bottom of the river, the electric eel contemplates the mottled bodies of piranha, amber stilts of wading birds. Unfazed and cherubic, a shy sun bittern sails between the open jaws of two jacaré. As the eel lifts its wide black head curiously out of the water we feel a little tingle in our fingertips, and the silvery lightning clouds of early evening begin to pile up like an elaborate hairdo, a black-edged invitation to storm. In pairs, parrots flee across the bruised and reddened lips of the rising moon. The forest is tinged crimson. Lit by firelight men on a remote white beach hunch over huge blackened pots, pound tapir flesh, grind ocelot bone. Skins are draped across bushes, and an overturned turtle feebly waves its pale, moonlit legs. The storm breaks. Eel submerges.

Aboard the Izabel Mariá

Cocooned in a fibrous hammock,
all night an elderly country woman
rolls and lights straw cigarettes, starts
imaginary fires.

❧

Metallic blue from beak to tip, hummingbird
navigates the Rio Amazonas, unfurls a rainbow
to startle the sky.

❧

Beware the flower of the cannonball tree—
too luridly red, too flamboyant:
dripping with bees.

❧

Beneath the rose-and-white striped awning
of the *Galeandra* orchid, someone waves
from the little opaque window.

❧

The trees, on their knees, twist in the wind.

❧

Our boat's owners, two brothers, tell the story
of their father, murdered by bandits on the river—
we drink the same riverwater, breathe the same apocryphal air.

Lizard

Looks like it swallowed a small frying pan.

Doesn't know how to use a parachute, can't be trained.

Tinted the shade of a bottle of bad castor oil.

Not a colour I would trust my life to.

Up and down its back blossom powder-grey lichens.

Prefers the brown overcoat to the blue one beneath.

Pale stripes along the tail lend it a certain savoir-faire.

The lizard that dwells at the base of my skull is other, is not brown.

Skitters from here to there, stone to rock.

Directs Lloyds of London from afar.

Lago Surubim

i

Below an enormous tree sit Paulo
and his family as though
suspended in the rising mist.
Hushed as in some great, remote cathedral.

A large smoke-grey hawk peers down,
prepared to pounce, then
dozens of tiny bats launch themselves upward
from blackened tree roots, spreading out
as an opened fan.

The hawk's death paces alongside
his appetite. Says, *but bats are not so nice as mice.*
(Death is getting anxious.)

ii

Each time we paddle by tall neon-green reeds
the sinewy necks of a dozen black ducks
follow us like periscopes. Some fly,
suspicious, bad-tempered,
interrupted at their morning meal.

In the mid-day shade
monkeys swing by, somersaulting
tree to tree, whistling shrilly for their pet dogs, lost
among the dusty leaves of the philodendron.

iii

Dressed in jet-black plumage,

ibis step solemnly along the swampy lakeside,
sickle bills doubled in the dark surface of the lake
like clusters of crescent moons.

Hawk flies up, Death riding him like a cowboy.

Galeandra

This one, lean as a whippet,
gossips instinctively, each flower
composed of five perked-up, canine ears,
thin and golden-brown, sensitive as radar.

Pouting maroon-and-white lips, dying to whisper,
That bee showed up next door again,
sex stirring all over its body, in and out
the front door of that brazen Catasetum...

Parana Anavilhanas

Fears rumours of leprosy, my pilot. Does not wish to linger
      on the south side of the river.
         Kite-tails of cloud explode with rain, blacker than obsidian.
            We travel from storm to storm.

With a shrill series of calls,
      a ringed kingfisher leads us
      to an igapó, a paradise
         of small delicate palms, egg-white beaches.

Insects conspire against me. When I paint an orchid,
      hordes of black flies descend. Pursued by irate wasps, I
         abandon an aroid. Charcoal burners devastate this lovely parana.
            I cannot wash the smell of smoke from my hair.

Fish Pictographs

Sticks, string, arrow

Too much anarchy, not enough fish

    ,think the fishermen

    They visualize little fish pictographs

    one fish skeleton equals
        two bowls peeled manioc
        one basket plantains
        a coiled liana

    not an orchid

Can the shaman?

        Yes, orchid
        Yes, even snake
        Whatever s/he desires

        Fish pictograph wriggles across her back

Lightning strikes, dynamite is the thunder:
        dead capybara, river turtle
        fish, fish, fish

Backwater, Little Bays

Day job
    scarlet leaves
    olive-green heart
    cling to a tree
    lure a botanist
then I'll flower

Night time
    lantern in the igapó
    the great Anaconda
    visits, licks the tiny
    white florets
wears them as a crown

Night time
    snake perfume, aphrodisiac
    they line up around
    the block: hawk-moths,
    praying mantis, night bees
wear them as a crown

Day job
    motionless for the portrait
    in a remote backwater
    on the Rio Urupadi
    transported to Rio for Carnival
then I'll flower

Encounters

i

The sound of hundreds of angel wings
beating simultaneously. Sumptuous.

Like the night in Manaus when nobody attended
the concert. We wore a footpath all around the *Teatro*
crooning Gilberto Gil to the marble busts and mango trees.

ii

I can't even see my hands in front of my face
trying to hum myself to sleep in the Óbidos Motel.

At daybreak everything is painfully bright,
hospital or asylum white.

iii

One afternoon wandering through Carnival in Rio
I was hypnotized. I tried on many styles of hat.

The knife-throwing man chose me as his target.
I was the best. I outshone all his minor stars.

On the Rio Trombetas

One eye of the maimed red and blue macaw sees more clearly
than my two

Bull's eye on the wooden table, bull's horns on the rough man
at the door

Cloying white orchid, sing your song, *Zygosepalum labiosum*

Crested iguanas basking in a tree, k-i-s-s-i-n-g

His best suit's jade and mother-of-pearl. *But the tail, you must
taste the tail*

Pendant moon gleams below gold-streaked clouds, pearls of
dawn, my frugal breakfast

Scowled at by rowdies, a spy from a mining company: yes,
that's me

My blackened sea: Henry Bates' glorious forest-covered lowlands

Flaming red bromeliad doesn't wish to leave its monkey cup tree

Beneath my petals, smoky purple, shelters dainty *Galeandra*

Jaguar, Lord of the Underworld, lay your paws delicately on me

No, I have not swum the choppy, shallow waters of Lake
Caipuru

Sketching late into the night, white bignone and I bloom under
moon's eye

Big snake owns bush, who owns the clusia flowers swaying in
    its crown

The strange swamp plant, *Rapatea*, thrives here, as would I,
    had I such roots

From the acacia tree, oropendola's throaty, musical riffs

Wild river goddess, urge your pink dolphins up the turbulent
    water

Notes:

NEAR THE SOLIMÕES RIVER, 1880

Tikuna body ornament, Museum für Völkerkunde, Vienna. Collected 1880. There are several species of cotinga (Family Cotingidae); this one is *Phoenicircus nigricollis*. Neotropical in distribution.

BOWL AND SPEAR

Tukano spear, collected circa 1830. Museum für Völkerkunde, Vienna. Double-headed jaguar bowl, lower Amazon, British Museum.

CASA DE PEDRA

Rock painting at Casa de Pedra, Alenquer, lower Amazon, Brazil. Date unknown. For Mary di Michele.

THE HOUSE OF THE TAPIR

Arumã is the common name for *Ischnosiphon spp.* in the arrowroot family Marantaceae, used by indigenous people in the northern Amazonian region to weave baskets and other items. For Lanny Brooks.

PACOVAL INCISED

Name for a decorative technique from near Lake Arari on Marajó Island, used on this turtle-shaped ceramic object (Musée Barbier-Mueller, Geneva). *Ceiba pentandra* (Family Bombacaceae) is commonly called the silk cotton tree. Kapok is made from its fruit fibers.

CHARM AGAINST PERSONAL FEARS

Jurupixuna tribal mask in bark cloth. Collected 1783-92 from the Amazon region by Alexandre Rodrigues Ferreira, a noted collector, natural historian, and artist. Museu Antropológico da Universidade de Coimbra.

FIRST CONTACT: SCISSORS

Pirarucú is a large green Amazonian river fish, *Arapaima gigas*, which can grow to 2 m. in length.

THE RAIN HOLDS ITS BREATH

Margaret Mee. *In Search of Flowers of the Amazon Forests.* 1988. Ed. T. Morrison. Nonesuch Expeditions Ltd., Suffolk, England. Journey one: 1956. To the River Gurupi. The painting (1959) is of the orchid *Gongora maculata* var. *bufonia* (also called *Gongora quinquenervis*). The flowers Mee heard opening were *Pseudobombax* sp.

FOR THE GIANT ANTEATER

Journey one. Candomblé is an African cult in Brazil whose practices include ritual sacrifice of cocks for certain ceremonies. Field sketch of *Gustavia augusta* (family Lecythidaceae) by Mee (1956); flowers are large with prominent orange-yellow centres. This large tropical tree family includes the brazil nut and cannonball trees. The lily is actually not a true lily, but the flower *Eucharis amazonica*. An igarapé is a small natural canal that may become dry seasonally.

RIO GUAMÁ
Rio Guamá forms the southern and western boundaries of the port city of Belém and empties into the Amazon. Mee visited Belém in 1956.

GUSTAVIA AUGUSTA
On the Rio Gurupi in Pará state in 1956 Mee first sketched *Gustavia augusta* and later did a formal painting.

MOON WITH ANT
The traditional Rikbaktsa territory in northern Mato Grosso State extended 50 thousand sq. km. On paper, as of 1998, they possessed 4 thousand sq. km. Their numbers were reduced from about 1300 in 1957 to 300 by 1969. They live in malocas (round communal houses) with roofs and walls of palm leaves. Famous for spectacular featherwork—necklaces, spears, headdresses, headbands, armbands, and nose pins—they use feathers from several species of macaw, as well as parakeets, curassows and guans. I wrote this poem in the Rikbaktsa language and then translated it into English.

ALTO JURUENA
Journey two: 1962. To 'the Denser Forest' The Mato Grosso. Mee called the rose-pink water plants by their common name, podostemons. They are in the family Podostemaceae which V.H. Heywood in *Flowering Plants of the World* describes as "a family of aquatic herbs resembling mosses." They are broadly distributed in the tropics and usually associated with fast flowing water.

THE RIKBAKTSA
Journey two. Mee very much admired the Rikbaktsa. The yellow-rumped cacique (*Cacicus cela*) builds purse-like nests and lives in colonies. Caboclo is the Portuguese name used for Amazonian descendants of mixed indigenous and Caucasian blood.

ARIPUANA
Journey two. *Oncidium cebolleta* is a Neotropical orchid.

BLUE SILK
Journey two.

AKA HEAVEN
Journey three: 1964. To 'the Far North.' The bromeliad is *Streptocalyx poeppigii*. Painted by Mee in 1985. The scarlet macaw, *Ara macao*, is often glimpsed in flocks and frequently feeds high in trees.

SERRA DO CURICURIARI
Journey three. Serra is Portuguese for mountain. The extravagantly coloured cock-of-the-rock (*Rupicola rupicola*) is a bird believed to have important spiritual significance to the Tucáno Indians in the region around Rio Curicuriari.

SMALL PINK NEBULAE
Journey three.

CLUSIA FIELD SKETCH
Mee sketched red flowers of *Clusia* sp, a tree in the cosmopolitan family Guttiferae, on the Uaupés River in 1964. Some *Clusia* species have been used as a source of healing gums.

KING OF THE AMAZON
Journey three. The clusia trees Mee noted, with "deep purple-bronze petals with lemon fringed centres," are not identified. The bushmaster, *Lachesis muta*, is the largest venomous snake in the Neotropics.

COMMODUS ON THE CAUABURI
Journey four: 1967. To 'the Mountains of Mist.' *Acacallis cyanea* is the rare blue orchid, collected and sketched by Mee in 1967 on the Rio Cauaburi. Commodus was an emperor who ruled Rome from 177-192.

MOUNTAIN OF MIST AND CLOUD
Journey four. During his years in the Amazon (1849-1864), the British botanist and explorer Richard Spruce heard rumours of the Mountain of Mist, but did not explore it. Members of the Waika tribe are now commonly known as Yanomami. Arara is Portuguese for macaw.

PICO DA NEBLINA
Journey four. The jaguar is the most important and most feared predator in this region. Feiticeiro is Portuguese for shaman.

WHY
Journey four. Mee and her companions did not reach the summit of the Mountain of Mist.

THE SANTA CASA
Journey five: 1967. To the 'Waika' Indians of the River Marauiá. *Catasetum saccatum* is a Neotropical orchid Mee sketched in 1967. The parrot, named Curica, was Mee's pet. For R.T.

THE MONKEY-SKIN BRACELET AND I
Journey five. The Waika made a dark dye from genipapo (or jenipapo), *Genipa americana* of the family Rubiaceae. It also apparently repels insects, and, when

used as decoration on skin, remains indelible for several days. Traditionally, among the Waika, the ashes of a dead person are ground to a powder, mixed with plantain, and made into soup to be eaten by the relatives.

THE CURIOUS WAISTCOAT OF THE ARMADILLO
Journey five. The trees are *Clusia grandifolia*, beautifully sketched by Mee in 1967 from flowers collected on the Rio Negro. Urucu is a scarlet or russet stain derived from the seeds of *Bixa orellana* and used to colour skin, hair and other objects.

VOICE OF FLOWERS
Journey six: 1970. To the 'Upper Amazons' and the Twin Rivers of Sorrow. Peixe-cachorro is the freshwater dogfish (*Rhaphiodon vulpinus*), thought to be exclusively Neotropical in distribution.

ORCHID AND SANDPIPER
Journey six. The green orchid (*Clowesia warczewitzii*) is rather rare; apparently not seen by botanists for over eighty years until Mee collected it from the Rio Araçá.

AMAZONIAN WHITES
Journey six. A man named Albino warned Mee against exploring the Rio Demini—he apparently had many indigenous people in debt-service there and didn't want witnesses of their criminal treatment.

CLUSIA SPECIES
Mee collected white flowers of *Clusia* species (so-called because it has not yet been identified to species) from the Alto Rio Negro and sketched them. Her formal painting is dated 1987.

UP THE RIO NEGRO
Journey six. Jacaré is the Portuguese common name for the caiman. There are two Amazonian species, the black caiman *Melanosuchus niger*, and the speckled caiman, *Caiman sclerops*. For Derek Charlwood.

FISH LEAP TOWARD THE MOON
Journey seven: 1971. To the River Maués and the Land of Guaraná. The tucanaré, or peacock bass (*Cichla ocellaris*) is an Amazonian fish, a common food item. The red-headed woodpecker could be any one of four species of *Campephilus*. A very agile forest carnivore in the family Mustelidae, the tayra (*Eira barbara*) is related to skunks, weasels and otters.

TRANSLATING YELLOWS

Journey eight: 1972. Through the Cradle of the Red Desert. The golden blossoms are flowers of a vine in the family Bignoniaceae that Mee sketched on the Rio Mamori. For Anne Halley.

MISTAKEN FOR THIEVES

Journey eight. Pau d'arco is the common name for Brazil's national tree, *Tabebuia serratifolia*.

CARNELIAN FLOWERS, DARK TREES

Journey eight. The bromeliad is *Billbergia decora*, collected and sketched on the Rio Cuinini in 1972, which empties into the Rio Negro not far from the town of Barcelos. The formal painting is dated 1978.

THE MARAÚ RIVER: A LAMENT

Journey eight. *Cecropia* is a genus of trees with large silvery-green leaves. It is one of the first types of vegetation to colonize newly-cleared land. Igapó is a forest that is naturally flooded by the rising annual waters of the Amazon. The painting is of a member of the Mauhés tribe by Alexandre Rodrigues Ferreira.

BIOGRAPHIES

Urospatha sagittifolia is an aroid, a common name for a large pantropical family of herbaceous plants. A spathe is a large sheath-like bract or leaf partly enclosing an inflorescence. Phloem is the portion of the vascular system in plants consisting of living cells arranged into elongated tubes that transport sugar and other nutrients throughout the plant. *Helicona* is an herbaceous Neotropical plant genus notable for its brightly-coloured bracts. *Heliconia chartacea* var. *meeana* was collected from Rio Uaupés. The orchid *Cattleya violacea* was first discovered by von Humboldt and Bonpland on the Rio Orinoco, Venezuela, in the 1800's. *Nymphaea rudgeana* is a night-blooming water lily, first described from Óbidos on the Rio Amazonas by Richard Spruce in 1849. *Scuticaria steelii* is a Neotropical orchid. The várzea is the land adjacent to a white water river flooded during the season of high water. *Philodendron brevispathum* is in the family Araceae. Mee painted *Cochleanthes brevispathum* (Family Orchidaeceae) in 1978. In Brazil, records indicate it is restricted to western Amazonas state.

GLORY

The River Amapari and the port of Santana are in Ampá state in northeastern Amazonian Brazil. The aroid known as aninga (*Montrichardia arborescens*) contains very poisonous latex (it can cause blindness), and is generally avoided. It sometimes grows in dense masses along river edges. This particular *Heliconia* species grows to several meters in height and its bracts are very large.

MARGARET CONSIDERS VON HUMBOLDT
The jambeiro tree (*Eugenia jambos*), which produces red edible fruit, is Asian in origin, but is now found in parts of the Amazon basin. The common name for the pink (or red) dolphin (*Inia geoffrensis*) is bôto. It is found only along the Amazon river and its tributaries. For Greville Mee.

NOTES FROM THE HOTEL PARIS, MANAUS
Journeys nine & ten: 1974 & 1975. An interlude with Friends. Mee's maps of each of her trips are remarkably accurate.

THE BAY OF SAPUCAIA
Journeys nine & ten. The hoatzin (*Opisthocomus hoazin*) nests along quiet forested streams and feeds exclusively on vegetation. For Ricardo Sternberg.

TO BE SUNG TO VILLA-LOBOS' "THE AMAZON FOREST"
Journeys nine & ten. Mee painted the flower of *Epidendron ciliare* to illustrate *Orchidaceae Brasilienses* by G.F.J. Pabst. The red cedar tree is in the family Meliaceae. Located on the south bank of the Rio Negro, Old Airão is an abandoned eighteenth-century Portuguese settlement. Heitor Villa-Lobos (1887-1959), was a revered Brazilian musician and educator.

WASPS
Journeys nine & ten. On several journeys Mee and her friends and guides were stung by various species of wasps. For David Homel.

FOUNTAINS OF WATER BLOWN SKYWARD
Journeys nine & ten.

WILDLIFE
Macaco-de-cheiro (*Saimiri sciureus*) is a small, playful monkey, generally with gold-coloured limbs, restricted to the Neotropics. Louis Agassiz (1807-1873) was a prominent Swiss naturalist and zoologist who founded the Museum of Comparative Zoology at Harvard. He is perhaps best-known for his work on fossil fish. He believed that people of African origin were less intelligent than other humans. The pygmy anteater (*Cyclopes didactylus*) was painted by Alexandre Rodrigues Ferreira. In the Emilio Goeldi Museo in Belém lives a black jaguar (*Panthera onca*). *Pteronura brasiliensis*, the giant otter, is in the family Mustelidae that also includes badgers, minks and weasels. The giant otter can grow to 1.8 m in length. The oropendola, *Psaracolius decumanus maculosus*, has a remarkable fluting call and lives communally in hanging straw nests.

Exceptionally striking visually, the hyacinth macaw, *Anodorhynchus hyacinthinus*, is nearly extinct from a combination of habitat loss and hunting for the exotic pet-store trade. For Phil Lounibos.

SEEKING THE SOURCE OF THE RIO CAUHY
Journey eleven: 1977. The Sad Fate of the Blue Qualea. Adolpho Ducke (1876-1959) was a highly respected Amazonian entomologist and botanist. He described in his notebooks what is believed to be a previously unrecorded species of the rare tree, *Qualea* (now *Erisma calcaratum*), found exclusively along the banks of the Rio Cauhy. Mee found only a shallow swamp in a devastated area—possibly the remains of the headwaters of the Cauhy.

EEL AND STORM
Journey eleven. The electric eel, *Electrophorus electricus*, is found in freshwater rivers in South America. It prefers murky water with a slow current, can reach 2.5 m in length and emit a shock of up to 600 V. *Eurypyga helias* is the sun bittern, inhabiting forested borders of marshes and streams in tropical Central and South America.

ABOARD THE IZABEL MARIÁ
Journey eleven. The cannonball tree is *Couroupita guianensis*. Mee painted *Galeandra devoniana* in 1985.

LIZARD
Mee. Field sketch, 1961.

LAGO SURUBIM
Journey twelve. 1982. The Cactus of the Flooded Forest.

GALEANDRA
Lake Caipuru was the source of Mee's 1984 sketch of the orchid *Galeandra*.

PARANA ANAVILHANAS
Journeys thirteen & fourteen. 1984. A 'Storm' on the River Trombetas. The ringed kingfisher is *Ceryle torquata*.

FISH PICTOGRAPHS
Journeys thirteen & fourteen.

BACKWATER, LITTLE BAYS
The subject is *Neoregelia eleutheropetala* (family Bromeliaceae), a widespread Amazonian bromeliad. Mee located this specimen on the Rio Urupadi in 1971, and completed the formal painting the same year.

ON THE RIO TROMBETAS

Journeys thirteen & fourteen. *Zygosepalum labiosum* has fragrant long-lasting flowers and is found in lowland forests. Mee's formal painting of this lovely orchid is dated 1976. Henry Bates, a prominent 19th century British naturalist, explored the Amazon basin for eleven years. The flaming bromeliad is *Streptocalyx poeppigii*, painted by Mee in 1985. Monkey cups are the empty fibrous fruits of the paradise nut tree, *Lecythis zabucajo*, closely related to the Brazil nut tree. The white bignone is a trumpet vine, *Phryganocydia corymbosa*, collected near the Rio Trombetas in 1984, the same year Mee painted it. The genus *Rapatea* includes several unusual-looking swamp plants. It is not known which species Mee described on this trip. Mee most probably saw (and heard) a crested oropendola, *Psarocolius decumanus*.

ANI TALKING (back cover)

Journeys thirteen & fourteen. 1984. The ani (*Crotophaga ani*) is a bird believed by some Brazilians to accompany the souls of the dead or to presage a death. Guariba is the common Portuguese name for the howler monkey (*Aluata*).

Selected Bibliography

Caufield, C. 1986. *In the Rainforest*. Pan Books, London.

Davis, W. 1996. *One River*. Simon & Schuster, New York.

Desowitz, R.S. 1997. *Who gave Pinta to the Santa Maria? Tracking the Devastating Spread of Lethal Tropical Diseases into America*. Harcourt Brace, San Diego, New York, London.

Elmquist, T., Cox, P.A., Rainey, W.E. and Pierson, E.D. 1992. Restricted pollination on oceanic islands: pollination of *Ceiba pentandra* by flying foxes in Samoa. *Biotropica* 24:15-23.

Emmons, L.H. 1990. *Neotropical Rainforest Mammals. A Field Guide*. The University of Chicago Press, Chicago and London.

Fleming, P. 1933. *Brazilian Adventure*. Penguin, Harmondsworth, England.

Forsyth A. and Miyata, K. 1984. *Tropical Nature*. Scribners, New York.

Galeano, E. 1984. *Memoria del Fuego. II. Las caras y las máscaras*. Siglo Veintiuno Editores, SA.

Gremone, C., Cervigón, F., Gorzula, S., Medina, G., and Novoa, D. *Fauna de Venezuela. Vertebrados*. Ed. Biosfera, S.R.L. Caracas, Venezuela.

Hatoum, M. 2000. *The Brothers*. Bloomsbury, London.

Hecht, S. and Cockburn, A. 1990. *The Fate of the Forest*. HarperCollins, New York.

Heywood, V.H. 1978. *Flowering Plants of the World*. Mayflower Books, New York.

Hoyos Fernandez, J. 1987. *Guia de Arboles de Venezuela*. Soc. Ciencias Naturales La Salle, Caracas, Venezuela.

Kandell, J. 1984. *Passage through El Dorado*. Avon Books, New York.

Kricher, J.C. 1989. *A Neotropical Companion*. Princeton University Press, Princeton, New Jersey.

Lévi-Strauss, C. *Tristes Tropiques*. 1955. Eng. Translation 1973, Jonathan Cape, London.

Lundberg, J. 2001. Freshwater Riches of the Amazon. *Natural History* 9:36-43.

McEwan, C., Barreto, C. and Neves, E. 2001. *Unknown Amazon*. The British Museum Press, London.

Mee, M. 1988. *Margaret Mee's Amazon*. Illustrated catalogue of paintings, text by Mayo, S. Royal Botanic Gardens, Kew.

Mee, M. 1988. *In Search of Flowers of the Amazon Forests.* Ed. Morrison, T. Nonesuch Expeditions Ltd., Suffolk, England.

Mee, M. 1996. *Margaret Mee, Return to the Amazon.* Ed. Stiff, R. Royal Botanic Gardens, Kew. The Stationary Office, London.

Mee, M. 2001. *The Amazon Collection: The Botanical Paintings of Margaret Mee.* BrasilConnects & Royal Botanic Gardens, Kew.

Mee, M. 2004. *Margaret Mee's Amazon. Diaries of an Artist Explorer.* Antique Collectors' Club in association with The Royal Botanic Gardens, Kew.

Museu Paraense Emilio Goeldi. 1999. *Arte da Terra: Resgate da Cultura Materiale e Iconográfica do Pará.* Belém: Edição SEBRAE.

Naples, V. L. 1999. Morphology, evolution and function of feeding in the giant anteater (*Myrmecophaga tridactyla*). *Journal of Zoology* 249: 19-41.

Page, P.K. 1987. *Brazilian Journal.* Lester & Orpen Dennys, Toronto.

Roosevelt, T. 1914. *Through the Brazilian Wilderness.* John Murray, London.

Schultes, R.E. 1988. *Where the Gods Reign.* Synergetic Press, Arizona & London.

Schultes, R.E. 1990. Margaret Mee and Richard Spruce. *The Naturalist* (London) 115: 146-148.

Sick, H. 1997. *Ornitologia Brasileira.* Editora Nova Fronteira, S.A.

Silveira, L., Rodrigues, F.H.G., Jacoma, A.T.D. and Diniz, J.A.F. 1999. Impact of wildfires on the megafauna of Emas National Park, central Brazil. *Oryx* 33: 108-114.

Spruce, R. 1908. *Notes of a Botanist on the Amazon & Andes.* Ed. Wallace, A.F. Macmillan and Co. Ltd., London. Vol. I and II.

Zotz, G. and Winter, K. 1994. Photosynthesis of a tropical canopy tree, *Ceiba pentandra*, in a lowland forest in Panama. *Tree Physiology* 14:1291-1301.

Margaret Mee (1909-1988)

was an extraordinarily gifted painter, naturalist and explorer. Trained as
an artist in Britain at the Camberwell School of Art, she moved to
Brazil with her husband Greville, a graphic artist, in 1952. She taught
art at the British School St. Paul's in São Paulo and began to sketch and
paint flowers, especially those in the Serra do Mar, the southern coastal
mountains. In 1960 she became the resident botanical artist at the São
Paulo Botanical Institute, where one of her primary responsibilities
was to illustrate a volume on bromeliads for the Institute's huge *Flora
Brasilica* project.

Her first trip to the Amazon region, to the Rio Gurupi, not
far from the port city of Belém, was in 1956. She made fourteen
subsequent trips to the Amazon, the last in 1988, sketching and
describing at least ten new species of orchids and bromeliads. She also
located a number of species that had not been collected since their
initial discoveries in the 19th century by the renowned naturalist and
explorer Alexander von Humboldt, and the British botanist Richard
Spruce.

She sketched only from living plants, and painted in gouache.
Her sense of composition, her technical acumen and her exceptionally
fine colour matches give her paintings tremendous vitality and depth.

She was the first botanical artist to begin to put exuberant
background details into her formal botanical paintings. These serve as
a reminder that whole ecosystems give rise to such diversity, species
richness, and the critical need to preserve this extraordinary heritage.
Because she made so many thorough explorations of different parts of
the Amazon, Mee was among the first to speak up about this dire need.

Ironically, after surviving more than a few perilous incidents in
Amazonia, Mee was killed in an auto accident while visiting Britain.
She had received many honours during her lifetime and the Audubon
Society posthumously named her one of the 100 most important
explorers of the twentieth century, but, despite noteworthy exhibitions
of her work in England, Brazil and the United States she is still no
household word.

Grateful acknowledgment is made to the editors of those publications in which the following poems originally appeared:

American Entomologist: Wasps
The Antigonish Review: Lizard, Lago Surubim, To be Sung to Villa-Lobos' "The Amazon Forest", Encounters, Amazonian Whites, The Monkey Skin Bracelet and I, Casa de Pedra, Fish Pictographs
Arc: Wildlife
Delirium Press (limited edition broadside): Eel and Storm, illustrated by Oriole Farb Feshbach.
Descant: Clusia field sketch, Galeandra, Orchid and Sandpiper
Event: Mistaken for Thieves, Translating Yellows
The Fiddlehead: Pico da Neblina, The Santa Casa, Voice of Flowers, The Maraú River: A Lament
The Malahat Review: Aripuana, King of the Amazon, The Curious Waistcoat of the Armadillo, Glory, Mountain of Mist and Cloud, On the Rio Trombetas
Poetry Ireland Review: Near the Solimões River 1880, Bowl and Spear
Prairie Fire: AKA Heaven, Fountains of Water Blown Skyward
Prism International: Rio Guamá, Biographies
Queen's Feminist Review: Notes from the Hotel Paris, Manaus; Margaret Considers von Humboldt
Room of One's Own: The Rain Holds its Breath, Alto Juruena

"The Monkey-Skin Bracelet and I" was broadcast on CBC's *All in a Week-end* in February, 2004. "The Santa Casa" and several selections from "Biographies" were broadcast on CFRC Radio at Queens' University, Kingston, Ontario in March, 2004. "*Clusia* field sketch" was broadcast on CBC Radio One's *Art Talks* in April, 2004. I am grateful to all producers and interviewers for their interest and enthusiasm. The poem "Aboard the Izabel Mariá" was exhibited in conjunction with Oriole Farb Feshbach's paintings in a show called <u>Painting & Poetry</u> at the Forbes Library of the Hosmer Art Gallery in Northampton, Massachusetts, June 2-29, 2005.

Thanks to Women's Studies at the University of Vermont for a travel grant in 2000 and to the Canada Council for a Senior Writing grant to work on the Margaret Mee poems during 2001.

I am indebted to Phil Lounibos who gave me my first copy of Mee's brilliant and inspiring book *In Search of Flowers of the Amazon Forests*. Christine Kowal Post's intuition was important during the early planning stages of the project. I am very grateful to Greville Mee and his wife Elisabeth for their generosity. During my visits to the Library and Archives at the Royal Botanic Gardens at Kew, Marilyn Ward and her staff were endlessly patient and helpful with my many queries concerning Margaret Mee and her work. I appreciate the support of Sir Peter Crane, Director of Royal Botanic Gardens at Kew, and I am grateful for his generous preface. At the São Paulo Botanical Gardens, I thank Maria Tomas for allowing me access to Margaret Mee's paintings of bromeliads from the Atlantic rainforest, and Anice Sallum for her hospitality and company in São Paulo. I am delighted to thank Oriole Farb Feshbach for her use of my poem to complement her painting. I'm very grateful to the members of the Amherst Poetry Seminar for their ears and eyes. For careful reading and comments I thank David Conn, Mary di Michele, Jane Munro, Carl Schlichting, Carolyn Smart, and Richard Summerbell. Thanks especially to Stan Dragland at Brick Books for his editorial acumen, generosity, and astute advice. I'm also grateful to Kitty Lewis for her warmth and enthusiasm, to Maureen Harris for her careful copy-editing and organizational skills, and to Alan Siu for the beautiful cover design.

Although Margaret Mee's sketchbooks and paintings are inspiring on many levels, her journals were more valuable for my poems. She was a gifted observer and a fine writer, curious about everything around her. I found her detailed descriptions compelling and powerful, and I hope these poems will contribute to rekindling an interest in her remarkable legacy.

Jan Conn was born and raised in Asbestos, Quebec and has since lived in Montreal, Vancouver, Toronto, Guatemala, Venezuela, Florida, and Vermont. Since 2002 she has been living in Great Barrington, Massachusetts. She received her Ph.D. in Genetics from the University of Toronto in 1987 and is presently a Research Scientist at the Wadsworth Center, New York State Department of Health, and Associate Professor in the Department of Biomedical Sciences at the School of Public Health at SUNY-Albany. She specializes in the genetics of mosquitoes that transmit human pathogens, especially malaria parasites, and has been travelling and conducting fieldwork in Latin America since 1973. She has published five previous books of poetry, most recently *Beauties on Mad River* (Véhicule, 2000). Her poems have appeared in many literary journals and anthologies and a selection of Amazonian poems won second prize in the CBC literary awards, 2003. For more information see www.janconn.com